The New York S   n the Cri

Henry George Stebbins Noble

Alpha Editions

This edition published in 2022

ISBN: 9789356784819

Design and Setting By

Alpha Editions

www.alphaedis.com

Email - info@alphaedis.com

Contents

INTRODUCTION

The year 1914 has no precedent in Stock Exchange history. At the present time (1915), when the great events that have come to pass are still close to us, even their details are vivid in our minds and we need no one to rehearse them. Time, however, is quick to dim even acute memories, and Wall Street, of all places, is the land of forgetfulness. The new happenings of all the World crowd upon each other so fast in the financial district that even the greatest and most far-reaching of them are soon driven out of sight. This being the case, it has seemed to the writer of these pages that some record should be kept among the brokerage fraternity of what was so great an epoch in their history, and that this record could best be written down by one who happened to be very favorably placed to know the story in its entirety.

Of course the archives of the Exchange will always contain the minutes of Committees and other documentary material embodying the story of the past, but this dry chronicle is never likely to see the light except when unearthed by law courts or legislative committees. It seems worth while, therefore, to disentangle the essential thread of the tale of 1914 from the mass of unreadable detail in the minute books, and put it in a shape where those who are interested may look it over.

This is not an easy task. To differentiate the interesting and the essential from the mass of routine material is, perhaps, not very difficult, but to present this segregated matter in a form that will not be monotonous is much more of a problem. The proceedings of a Committee that has been in continuous session must, when written down, partake of the nature of a diary, and to that extent be tiresome reading. We shall, therefore, have to ask the indulgence of any one who happens to look into these pages, and beg him to pass over the form for the sake of the substance. That the substance itself is of deep interest goes without saying. It was given to the Stock Exchange to play a great part in a momentous world crisis, and it must be of profound interest to know how that part was played.

Stock Exchanges are a relatively recent product of modern civilization, and like new comers in every field they are suspected and misunderstood. The most complex of all problems are economic problems, and the functions of Stock Exchanges form a most intricate part of political economy. It has, consequently, been a noticeable phenomenon in all contemporary industrial society that the activities of the stock markets have been a constant subject of agitation and legislative meddling. Most of this meddling has been based upon ignorance and misunderstanding, but in a broad view this ignorance and misunderstanding are excusable owing to the novelty and above all the great complexity of the factors at work. One of the needs of the time, therefore, is that the public, and their representatives in the Legislatures, should be enlightened as fast as possible with regard to the immensely important uses of these institutions, and to the operation of their very delicate machinery.

The World crisis of 1914 forced upon us an object lesson on the question of speculative exchanges in general which ought to be of lasting profit. For years agitators had been hard at work all over the country urging the suppression of the Cotton Exchanges, and claiming that they contained gamblers who depressed the price of the cotton growers' product. In the summer of 1914 the dreams of these agitators were realized. The Cotton Exchanges were all closed and the cotton grower was given an opportunity of testing the benefits of a situation where there was no reliable agency to appraise the value of cotton. The result may be summed up in the statement that the reopening of the Cotton Exchanges met with no opposition. A similar object lesson was furnished in the case of the Stock Exchanges. They were all closed, and for a few weeks some profound thinkers in the radical press stated that the country was showing its ability to dispense with them. When the time for their reopening came, however, there was no agitation to prevent it. On the contrary it was hailed as a sign of the resumption of normal financial conditions in the United States.

This evidence that the experience of 1914 has cast a much needed light on the public value of speculative exchanges, gives a further excuse for describing in some detail how the experience was passed through by that greatest of all these institutions, the New York Stock Exchange.

The New York Stock Exchange
CHAPTER I

THE CLOSING OF THE EXCHANGE

The Stock Exchange is in the second century of its existence and in that long period of time (long relatively to the number of years during which Stock Exchanges have been known to the world) it has been forced to close its doors only twice. The first occasion was the great panic of 1873, the after effect of civil war when trading was suspended for ten days; the second came with the outbreak of the world War in the close of July, 1914. These two remarkable events differ profoundly in the gravity of the circumstances which brought them about. In 1873, although the financial disturbance was one of the greatest the United States has ever experienced, the trouble was mainly local and did not seriously involve the entire world. The Exchange was not closed in anticipation of a catastrophe but was obliged to shut down after the crash had taken place, in order to enable Wall Street to gather up its shattered fragments. The measure of this crisis was the ten days during which trading was suspended.

Far different from these were the circumstances surrounding July 31st, 1914. On that eventful date a financial earthquake of a violence absolutely without precedent shook every great center of the civilized world, closing their markets one by one until New York, the last of all, finally suspended in order to forestall what would have surely been a ruinous collapse. The four and a half months during which this suspension continued stand to the ten days closing of 1873 in a proportion which fitly illustrates the relative gravity of the two historic upheavals.

In the light of these facts we are justified in asserting that the events of 1914 are the most momentous that have so far constituted the life and history of the New York Stock Exchange, and consequently that some record of, and commentary upon, these facts may be of value to the present members of that body and of interest and profit to its future members.

It is in the nature of panics to be unforeseen, but the statement may be truly made that some of them can be more unforeseen than others. The panic of 1907 was preceded by anxious forebodings in the minds of many well informed people, whereas the Venezuela panic in 1895, being due to the sudden act of an individual, came out of a clear sky. To the latter class distinctively belongs the great convulsion of 1914. While the standing armies of Europe were a constant reminder of possible war, and the frequent diplomatic tension between the Great Powers cast repeated war shadows over the financial markets, the American public, at least, was entirely unprepared for a world conflagration. Up to the final moment of the launching of ultimata between the European governments no one thought it possible that all our boasted bonds of civilization were to burst over night and plunge us back into mediæval barbarism. Wall Street was therefore taken unaware, and so terrific was the rapidity with which the world passed, in the period of about a week, from the confidence of long enduring peace to the frightful realization of strife, that no time was given for men to collect their thoughts and decide how to meet the on-rushing disaster.

Added to the paralyzing effect of this unheard of speed of action, there came the disconcerting thought that the conditions produced were absolutely without precedent. Experience, the chart on which we rely to guide ourselves through troubled waters, did not exist. No world war had ever been fought under the complex conditions of modern industry and finance, and no one could, for the moment, form any reliable idea of what would happen or of what immediate action should be taken. These circumstances should be kept clearly in mind by all who wish to form a clear conception of this great emergency, and to estimate fairly the conduct of the financial community in its efforts to save the day.

The conditions on the Stock Exchange, when the storm burst, were in some respects very helpful. Speculation for several years had been at a low ebb, so that values were not inflated nor commitments extended. Had such a war broken out in 1906, with the level of prices then existing, one recoils at the thought of what might have happened. Furthermore, the unsettled business outlook due to new and untried legislation had fostered a heavy short interest in the market, thereby furnishing the best safeguard against a sudden and disastrous drop. This short interest was a leading factor in producing the extraordinary resistance of prices in New York which caused so much favorable comment during the few days before the closing. It were well if ill-informed people who deprecate short selling would note this fact.

During the week preceding July 31st, therefore, in the face of a practical suspension of dealings in the other world markets, the New York market stood its ground wonderfully. The decline in prices, though it became violent on July 30th, showed no evidence of collapse. There was a continuous market everywhere up to the last moment, and call money was obtainable at reasonable prices. Here was a perplexing problem when the closing of foreign Bourses raised the question of how long we should strive to keep our own Exchange open.

To close the recognized public market for securities, the market which is organized and safeguarded and depended upon as a standard of values, is an undertaking of great responsibility in any community. To take this step in New York, which is one of the four preeminent financial centers of the world, involved a responsibility of a magnitude difficult adequately to estimate. Upon the continuity of this market rest the vast money loans secured by the pledge of listed securities; numberless individuals depend upon it in times of crisis to enable them to raise money rapidly by realizing on security investments and thus safeguarding other property that may be unsaleable; the possessor of ready money looks to it as the quickest and safest field in which to obtain an interest return on his funds; and the business world as a whole depends upon it as a barometer of general conditions.

Add to this the fact that speculative commitments by individuals from all over the world, which have been based upon the expectation of an uninterrupted market, are left in hopeless and critical suspense if this market is suddenly removed, and it becomes apparent that to close the Exchange is manifestly to inflict far-reaching hardship upon vast numbers of people. It is also sure to be productive of much injustice. In bad times sound and solvent firms are anxious to enforce all their contracts promptly so as to protect themselves against those that are overextended; an obligatory suspension of business compels these solvent firms, in many cases, to help carry the risks of the insecure ones and deprives the provident man of the safety to which he is entitled.

When such facts as these are duly weighed by the agencies having the authority to close the stock market, it becomes clear that duty dictates a policy of hands off as long as a continuous market persists and purchasers continue to buy as the decline proceeds. This was well illustrated in the acute panic of 1907 when an enormous open market never ceased to furnish the means by which needy sellers constantly liquidated, and the possessors of savings made most profitable investments. To have closed the Exchange during that crisis—assuming it to have been possible—would have been an unmixed evil. The violent decline in prices was the natural and only remedy for a long period of over-speculation, and it would have been worse had it been artificially postponed.

Considerations of this general character, up to July 30th, caused the authorities of the New York Stock Exchange to take no action, although the other world markets had all virtually suspended dealings. On July 30th, the evidences of approaching panic showed themselves. An enormous business was done accompanied by very violent declines in prices, and, although money was still obtainable throughout the day, at the close of business profound uneasiness prevailed.

On the afternoon of July 30th, the officers of the Stock Exchange met in consultation with a number of prominent bankers and bank presidents, and the question of closing the Exchange was anxiously discussed. While the news from abroad was most critical, and the day's decline in prices was alarming, it was also true that no collapse had taken place and no money panic had yet appeared. The bankers' opinion was unanimous that while closing was a step that might become necessary at any time, it was not clear that it would be wise to take it that afternoon, and it was agreed to await the events of the following day. Meanwhile, several members of the Governing Committee of the Exchange had become convinced that closing was inevitable and, in opposition to the opinion of the bankers, urged that immediate steps be taken to bring it about. It may seem strange to people outside of Wall Street that the night before the Exchange closed such apparent indecision and difference of opinion existed. It was, however, a perfectly natural outcome of an unprecedented situation. The crisis had developed so suddenly, and the conditions were so utterly without historic parallel, that the best informed men found themselves at a loss for guidance.

During the evening of July 30th the conviction that closing was imperative spread with great speed among the large brokerage firms. Up to a late hour of the night the President of the Exchange was the recipient of many messages and telegrams from houses not only in New York, but all over the country, urging immediate action. The paralysis of the world's Stock Exchanges had meanwhile become general. The Bourses at Montreal, Toronto and Madrid had closed on July 28th; those at Vienna, Budapest, Brussels, Antwerp, Berlin, and Rome on July 29th; St. Petersburg and all South American countries on July 30th, and on this same day the Paris Bourse was likewise forced to suspend dealings, first on the Coulisse and then on the Bourse itself. On Friday morning, July 31st, the London Stock Exchange officially closed, so that the resumption of business on that morning would have made New York the only market in which a world panic could vent itself.

The Governing Committee of the Exchange were called to meet at nine o'clock (the earliest hour at which they could all be reached, for it was summer and many were out of town) and at that hour they assembled in the Secretary's office ready to consider what action should be taken. In addition to the Committee many members of prominent firms appeared in the room to report that orders to sell stocks at ruinous prices were pouring in upon them from all over the world and that security holders throughout the country were in a state of panic. It would be hopeless to try to describe the nervous tension and excitement of the group of perhaps fifty men who consulted together under the oppressive consciousness that within forty-five minutes (it was then a quarter past nine) an unheard of disaster might overtake them. It was determined that the Governing Committee should go into session at once as there was so little time to spare. Just as they started for their official meeting room a telephone message was received from a prominent banking house stating that the bankers and bank presidents were holding a consultation and suggesting that the Exchange authorities await the conclusion of their deliberations.

There is an employee of the Exchange whose duty it is to ring a gong upon the floor of the big board room at ten o'clock in the morning. Until that gong has rung the market is not open and contracts are not recognized. This employee was instructed not to ring the gong until he had received personal orders to do so from the President; a permanent telephone connection was established with the office in which the bankers were conferring, and amid a horrible suspense the outcome of their conference was awaited. For twenty minutes this strain continued. It was a quarter before ten and only fifteen minutes remained in which to act. Meanwhile the brokers were fast assembling upon the board room floor, orders were piling in upon them to sell at panic prices, ten o'clock was approaching, and although all felt that the opening should not be permitted no one had a word from the Governing Committee as to what was going to be done.

———

At a quarter of ten, no word having come from the bankers, the receiver of the telephone which had been connected with their meeting place was hung up, and the Governing Committee were called in session to take action. As they took their seats two messages reached them. One was brought by a prominent member of their body who had gone to the office of the President of the bank Clearing House and had been told by him, after consulting with some of his fellow officers, "We concur; under no circumstances is it our suggestion, but if the Exchange desires to close, we concur." The other was sent, through a member of the Exchange, from one of the leading bank Presidents who stated that closing would be a grave mistake and that he was opposed to it.

The roll was called and thirty-six out of the forty-two members answered to their names. The Chair having announced the purpose of the meeting, Mr. Ernest Groesbeck moved that the Exchange be closed until further notice. This motion was carried, not unanimously but by a large majority. Mr. Groesbeck then moved that the delivery of securities be suspended until further notice, and, this being carried unanimously, made a third motion that a special Committee consisting of four members of the Governing Committee and the President be appointed to consider all questions relating to the suspension of deliveries and report to the Governing Committee at the earliest possible moment. The third motion, like the second was carried unanimously and the Committee adjourned. It was then four minutes of ten. On the instant that the first motion closing the Exchange was passed, word was sent to the ticker operators to publish the news on the tape. In this way the seething crowd of anxious brokers on the floor got word of the decision before ten o'clock struck. Immediately upon the adjournment of the Committee Mr. George W. Ely the Secretary of the Exchange ascended the Chairman's desk in the board room and made the formal announcement, which was greeted with cheers of approbation. The President promptly appointed Messrs. H. K. Pomroy, Ernest Groesbeck, Donald G. Geddes, and Samuel F. Streit to constitute, with himself, the Committee of Five, and the long suspense and anxiety of four months and a half began.

These events, which were crowded into a few feverish hours, and which seemed to those who participated in them more like a nightmare than like a reality, present some aspects that are especially worthy of detailed description. It is noticeable that the vote to close the Exchange was not unanimous. This shows the immense complexity of a situation, which, even at the last moment, left some two or three conscientious men undecided. It is a fact of profound importance, and one that never should be forgotten by stock brokers or by the public, that the Exchange closed itself on its own responsibility and without either assistance or compulsion from any outside influence. Many false assertions by professional enemies of the institution have been made to the effect that the banks forced the closing, or that its members were unwillingly coerced by outside pressure. The facts are that the influential part of the membership, the heads of the big commission houses, made up their minds on the evening of July 30th that closing was imperative, and that on the morning of July 31st their representatives in the Governing Committee took the responsibility into their own hands, the bankers having been unable as yet to reach a conclusion.

Immediately after the closing the President of the Exchange visited the prominent bank president who had served notice at the last moment of his disapproval of this procedure. He was found in his office in consultation with a member of one of the great private banking houses. Both the bank president and the private banker agreed that, in their opinion, the closing had been a most unfortunate mistake. It was an opportunity thrown away to make New York the financial center of the world. The damage was done and would have to be made the best of, but had the market been allowed to open the banks would have come to the rescue and all would have gone well. These gentlemen admitted that the Exchange was to some extent excusable owing to the negligence of the bankers in not notifying them that they were ready to protect the money market.

It may safely be stated that within twenty-four hours after this interview neither the two bankers in question nor any one else in Wall Street entertained these opinions. The rise of exchange on London to $7—a rate never before witnessed; the marking of the Bank of England's official discount rate to 10%, accompanied by a run on that institution which resulted in a loss of gold in one week of $52,500,000; the decline of the Bank's ratio of reserve from the low figure of 40% to the paralyzing figure of 14-5/8%; together with the fact that the surplus reserves of our New York Clearing House banks fell $50,000,000 below their legal requirements, were reasons enough in themselves to convince the most skeptical of the necessity of what had been done.

The frightful gravity of the situation which had arisen became clearer and more defined in people's minds a few days after the first of August than it was on the morning of July 31st. European selling had been proceeding for some time before the outbreak of War and in the last few days before closing had been temporarily arrested by the prohibitive level of exchange and the risk of shipment at sea. The American public itself, however, was seized with panic on the evening of July 30th, and on the morning of July 31st brokers' offices were flooded with orders to sell securities for what they would bring and without reference to values. Had the market been permitted to open on that Friday morning the familiar Wall Street tradition of "Black Friday" would have had a meaning more sinister than ever had been dreamed of before.

In all previous American panics the foreign world markets were counted upon to come to the rescue and break the fall. Imports of gold, foreign loans, and foreign buying were safeguards which in past crises had been counted upon to prevent utter disaster. On this occasion our market stood by itself unaided; an unthinkable convulsion had seized the world; panic had spread; even the bargain hunter was chilled by the unprecedented conditions; there were practically no buyers. A half hour's session of the Exchange that morning would have brought on a complete collapse in prices; a general insolvency of brokerage houses would have forced the suspension of all business; the banks, holding millions of unsaleable collateral, would have become involved; many big institutions would have failed and a run on savings banks would have begun. It is idle to speculate upon what the final outcome might have been. Suffice it to say that these grave consequences were prevented in the nick of time by the prompt and determined action of the Stock Exchange, and by that alone.

Any decisive step whether right or wrong always finds its critics. There were a few people who criticised the Exchange for closing too soon and thought that the feeling of panic was increased by this action. These few were mostly converted from their opinions as the situation became clearer. There was a larger number who took the ground that the Exchange had not closed soon enough, and urged that had the step been taken a few days sooner a considerable decline in values would have been prevented. It is strange that the latter critics did not stop to reflect on how great an advantage it was, all through the anxious days of August, to have had the New York market liquidated as far as it could be without disaster, and the level of closing prices relatively low. How vastly greater would have been the task of safeguarding the situation in the face of declining prices in the "New Street Market" had the closing prices on the Exchange been ten or fifteen points higher. The truth is that the Exchange was closed at the very best possible moment. The market was kept open as long as liquidation could safely be carried on (thus immensely diminishing the pressure to be withstood during the suspension) and it was closed at the very instant that a collapse was threatened.

The above facts suggest some reflections with regard to the agitation for governmental interference with or control of the Exchange. The act of closing necessitated the prompt decision of men thoroughly familiar with the circumstances in a period of time actually measured by minutes. If it had been necessary to reach government officials unfamiliar with details, convince them of the necessity of action, and overcome the invariable friction of public machinery, the financial world would have been prostrated before the first move had been made. If the Exchange had been an incorporated body, and had been closed in the face of the difference of opinion and possible conflict of interests that existed at the time, it would have been possible for a temporary injunction to have been brought against its management restraining its freedom to meet the emergency. Long before the merits of such an injunction could have been argued in court the harm would have been done, and ruin would have overtaken many innocent people. The full power of a group of individuals thoroughly familiar with the conditions to act without delay or restraint prevented a calamity which can safely be described as national.

It is a fact, which will probably never be appreciated outside of the immediate confines of Wall Street, that the Exchange was unexpectedly thrown into a position where the interests of the whole country were put in its hands, and that through the prompt and energetic action of the thirty-six men who faced the awful responsibility on July 31st financial America was saved. It is true that in saving the community they saved themselves, but so do the soldiers who win upon the battle-field, and in neither case is the obligation cancelled by the selfish considerations involved. When in future the perennial outcry against the Exchange is being fostered by those whose minds are exclusively occupied with the evils that are inseparable from every human institution, let us hope that once in a while some friendly voice may be raised to remind the world of July thirty-first, nineteen hundred and fourteen.

CHAPTER II

THE PERIOD OF SUSPENSION

During the same morning on which the momentous action of closing was taken the Committee of Five met and elected the President of the Exchange as their Chairman. The acute crisis was over, the danger of a cataclysm had been averted, but the situation that remained was big with problems full of menace and uncertainty.

Just what effect the closing of the market would have was a matter of doubt. On all previous occasions when the facilities of the Exchange had been inadequate, or had been shut off, an unregulated market had established itself in public places and proceeded uncontrolled. Thus during the Civil War, when the volume of speculation had completely outgrown the limited machinery of the old Board of Brokers, a continuous market developed partly in the street and partly in a basement room called the "Coal Hole" and flourished during the day, while in the evening it was continued in the lobby of the Fifth Avenue Hotel. This market did more business than was done upon the Exchange itself, and a few years after the War, many of its members, who had organized into the "Open Board of Brokers," were admitted to the Stock Exchange in a body. The suspension of business in 1873 was too brief to allow of the formation of a market such as the above, but, while it continued, cash transactions for securities were being carried on every day in the financial district.

Would results such as these obtain on this occasion? Much depended upon the length of time before the Exchange could re-open, but this in itself was a problem for which no one could venture a solution. Again, a vast volume of contracts made on July 30th had been suspended. How long could the enforcement of these contracts be successfully prohibited, and above all how long would the banks and financial institutions which were lending money on Stock Exchange collateral refrain from calling loans when they were deprived of any measure of the value of their security? Over its own members the New York Stock Exchange might exercise a rigid control, and it could safely be assumed that the other Stock Exchanges of the country would coöperate with it, but numberless outside agencies existed such as independent dealers unaffiliated with exchanges, and auctioneers, any of whom might establish a market. If declining prices were made through media of this description, and the press felt called upon to furnish them to the public, the closing of the Exchange might not suffice to prevent panic and disaster.

Oppressed by these considerations, and by an appalling sense of responsibility, the new Committee of Five began its labors in the morning of July 31st. The first step decided upon was to communicate with the Bank Clearing House Committee. Mr. Francis L. Hine, President of the Clearing House, was invited to meet the Committee of Five which he did, a little later in the day, and presented to them the following statement of the action taken by the Clearing House.

> "There was a meeting of the Clearing House Committee this morning in view of the closing of the New York Stock Exchange. It was the opinion of the Committee that the business and financial condition of New York and the entire country was sound but that the situation in Europe justified extreme prudence and self-control on the part of the United States; that the closing of the Stock Exchange was a wise precaution by reason of the disposition of all Europe to make it the market for whatever it wished to sell, and that in this country there was no occasion for any serious interruption of the regular course of business, either financial or mercantile."

After the retirement of Mr. Hine, the Chairman of the Committee on Clearing House of the Exchange stated that all the checks given to the Clearing House had been certified, and a notice was thereupon sent out instructing members to call for their drafts at the usual hour. Thus all the differences due on the day's transactions of July 30th were settled, and a first encouraging step was taken. It was also decided to permit the offering of call money on the floor of the Exchange.

The Committee held its second meeting on August 1st and the first of the long series of problems growing out of the closing of the market was at once presented to it. A letter from a brokerage house doing business with Europe was received in which it was pointed out that "arbitrageurs" who had sold stocks in New York and bought them in London during the previous fortnight had made their deliveries by borrowing stock in New York; that the stock purchased in London was due to arrive on this side, and that the usual process of financing it by returning the previously borrowed stock had been cut off through the suspension of unfulfilled contracts. This was likely to lead to very grave embarrassment because call money had practically disappeared and houses to whom this foreign stock was consigned might not be able to meet their obligation to pay for it as it arrived. There being no arrivals of foreign stock expected that day, the Committee deferred action, and thus gained time to think out ways and means of meeting the difficulty.

The second problem presented came in the form of a request for permission to sell securities outside of the Exchange. The firm of S. H. P. Pell & Co. had suspended, and a house which had been lending them money wished to be authorized to sell out the collateral. This was the first of many cases brought before the Committee, during its long tenure of office, in which individuals sought for a special privilege to sell securities they were anxious to market while trading in general was forbidden. In this case the applicants were referred to that section of the Constitution of the Exchange in which it is provided that members having contracts with insolvents shall close out these contracts in the Exchange when the securities involved are listed. The Exchange being closed, this provision answered the question without necessitating any independent action on the part of the Committee.

From the moment of the closing of the Exchange a growing pressure arose to determine just when and how it should be re-opened. The desire for information on this point was widespread, and when the gravity of the situation became clearer to the community, a great anxiety developed that the re-opening should, above all, not be premature. Realizing that the fear of sudden and ill considered action on this question was becoming dangerous to the restoration of confidence, the Committee of Five, at its meeting of August 3rd authorized the following statement.

> "Announcement is made by the President of the Stock Exchange, in answer to inquiries as to when the Exchange will open, that ample notice of such opening will be given."

In spite of this notice fear that the Stock Exchange might act injudiciously lingered for some time longer until the constant reiteration by its officers of their intention to act only in conjunction and in consultation with the banks permanently allayed it.

By Monday, August 3rd, a steady stream of letters had begun to pour in upon the Committee asking advice and direction upon any number of questions raised by the closing of the market, and offering every kind of suggestion and advice. In addition to this it soon became evident that interviews would have to be held with large numbers of people for the purpose of securing their cooperation, influencing their conduct, and obtaining information. The resolution of the Governing Committee by virtue of which the Committee of Five was brought into being merely stated that questions such as these should be considered and reported back "at the earliest possible moment." Clearly here was an impossible situation. The immense detail of the work which was beginning to unfold itself could never be handled by so large a body as the Governing Committee itself. Realizing that this difficulty must be met without a moment's delay the Committee of Five requested the calling of a special meeting of the Governors for twelve o'clock the same day and presented to them the following resolution, which was unanimously adopted.

> "RESOLVED: That the Special Committee of Five, appointed by the Governing Committee on July 31st, be, and it hereby is, authorized during the present closing of the Exchange, to decide all questions relating to the business of the Exchange and its members."

This action of the Governing Committee, while it was rendered necessary by the peculiar requirements of the situation, was unprecedented in the history of the Exchange, for never before had such powers and such responsibilities been put in the hands of so few individuals. It was one of a series of "war measures" by means of which ends were achieved that would not have been reached in any other way.

Clothed with complete authority the Committee met again in the afternoon of August 3rd and was at once confronted with a request for a ruling on the question of how far members were to be restrained from dealing outside of the Exchange. After a lengthy discussion the following was approved as their opinion.

> "It was the intention in closing the Stock Exchange that trading should be stopped and it is the duty of loyal members to comply. If cases come into your office where it is absolutely necessary to trade, do so as quietly as possible and prevent the quotation from being published."

It will be noticed that the policy adopted here was less stringent than what came later when the growth of an outside market increased the dangers of the situation.

With the question of outside dealings there at once arose the closely connected question of the danger arising from having price quotations of such dealings made public. The quotation machinery of the Exchanges had been silenced by the closing of those institutions, but there remained the public auctioneers whose sales, if they took place, would be disseminated by the press and might spread panic among security holders and money lenders. The auctioneers in New York, Boston, Philadelphia, and Chicago were at once approached, not only directly but through their bankers and other advisers. It was a disagreeable task as these auctioneers had to be urged to cease doing business, but it was rendered unexpectedly easy by the courtesy and friendliness with which they coöperated for the general welfare. So loyal were these various agencies that not a single sale, either of listed or unlisted securities, occurred in any auction room of the country until the urgent phases of the crisis had passed.

It was not in auction rooms alone, however, that prices might be made; dealings were liable to occur in any unexpected locality, and it was urgent that prices of an alarming character should be kept from the public. For this most important purpose the coöperation of the press was absolutely necessary. To obtain this, at the outset, was no easy matter. The closing of the Stock Exchange placed the financial news writers of the daily press in a curious position. With them were allied that group of financial writers connected with the various Wall Street news agencies, the several financial journals that are exclusively devoted to Wall Street affairs, and the financial correspondents of out of town newspapers. All told there were about one hundred salaried men in these various groups, men experienced in financial affairs, widely known and respected, engaged in a work which had never been interrupted and which, as far as could be foreseen, promised to furnish them with a continuous vocation.

The first effect of the war was a general curtailment of newspaper advertising, a rise in the price of paper, and a greatly increased cost of the news of the day owing to excessive cable charges for foreign dispatches. Thus the newspapers suffered a rapidly diminishing revenue, and they found it necessary to discharge many of their employees and to reduce the salaries of others. With the Stock Exchange closed, naturally the salaried financial writers were among the first to feel this hardship.

Those whose services were retained throughout this crisis were confronted with divided responsibilities. It was their duty to interpret a mass of more or less fantastic rumors at a time when nerves were overwrought and points of view magnified and distorted. They wished to prevent the publication of anything of an incendiary nature, while at the same time a necessity arose for presenting to the public the news to which it was entitled. Placed in such a position there was a very natural impatience here and there to have the Exchange reopened, while now and then a tendency became manifested to publish certain news of the day which, while interesting to the public, tended to handicap the efforts of those bent only on reassurance and calm counsel. At times it became somewhat difficult to prevent the publication of some of these matters, particularly of the prices made in the so called "gutter" market which sprang up in New Street. And yet on the whole nothing could have exceeded the fairness and the spirit of coöperation of these gentlemen in this trying time. One newspaper even went so far as to cease the publication of a remunerative page of small advertisements having to do with dealings in outside securities. This was done at the request of the Committee without hesitation. Others coöperated in the suppression of advertising on the part of questionable people, while correspondents of out of town newspapers, both foreign and domestic, cheerfully acceded to requests to suppress all disturbing financial reports. In a word, the financial department of the whole newspaper press accepted the situation philosophically, bearing their losses without complaint and supporting without cavil the restrictive measures which it was necessary to employ.

This loyal conduct of the press and of the auctioneers was one of the great factors without which the critical days of the suspension of business could not have been successfully surmounted.

It will be remembered that in the morning of July 31st, the Governing Committee not only voted to close the Exchange but also declared that the delivery of securities should be suspended until further notice. The motive of this latter action was to prevent the possible insolvencies that were likely to be forced if purchasers were compelled to pay for their securities in the absence of a call money market. At the earliest moment that attention could be given to it the Committee of Five requested the Chairman of the Stock Exchange Clearing House to place before it the exact figures of the outstanding contracts. These figures when presented showed that there were stock balances open on Clearing House order amounting to $38,700,000 and Ex-Clearing House contracts amounting to about $61,000,000. Roughly speaking there had been about $100,000,000 of stock sold in the Exchange on July 30th, the delivery of which to the purchasers had been suspended by the action of the Governing Committee. Obviously a first great step toward clearing up the situation and preparing the ground for the ultimate reopening of the market was to get this great volume of contracts settled, so that if any failures were inevitable they would be disposed of beforehand.

It being probable that many of the purchasers of stock on July 30th were in a position to finance their purchases even in the midst of the crisis the Committee deemed it wise to offer every possible facility for the immediate settlement of contracts when the purchaser was in this position. They therefore issued the following notice on August 4th:

> "The Special Committee of Five appointed to consider questions connected with the closing of the Exchange state that the resolution of the Governing Committee suspending deliveries until further notice does not mean

that settlement may not be made by mutual consent wherever feasible. The Clearing House of the Exchange is prepared to advise and assist, and inquiries should be made in person there."

At the request of the Committee of Five the Committee on Clearing House at once undertook the task of assisting members of the Exchange in closing up these contracts and used its clerical force for that purpose, thus involving much careful and detailed work. They held daily continuous meetings, giving their personal attention in assisting members, and using a care that involved both tact and arduous labor. Through their efforts such extraordinary progress was made, in this complex and difficult task, that by September 22nd announcement was made that the delivery of all Clearing House balances had been completed with the exception of those of the few firms whose affairs were in the hands of receivers. These were settled shortly afterwards and at the same time the great volume of Ex-Clearing House contracts were also completely fulfilled.

This is one of the most extraordinary and gratifying experiences of the great crisis. In about seven weeks, at a time when money was unobtainable and the condition of panic was at its height, this huge volume of unsettled contracts was met and consummated by voluntary coöperation and without compulsion of any kind. In some few cases selfishness or indifference delayed action on the part of individuals, but these were all brought to a final adjustment by the influence and persuasion of the Committee.

This achievement not only reflects undying credit upon the members of the Exchange by showing both the sound condition of their business and their zeal to act for the general welfare, and creates a deep sense of obligation to the Clearing House Committee who for many long weeks worked unceasingly to overcome the difficulties that beset the path, but it justifies and confirms the wisdom of the New York Stock Exchange in adhering to the practice of daily settlements. In all the great European centers, where trading on the fortnightly settlement basis is in vogue, the restoration of dealings was terribly complicated by the herculean task of clearing up back contracts that extended over many days. In New York, when conditions so shaped themselves as to warrant reopening the Exchange, the back contracts of its members had all been settled up *two months* before. Had our system, like the European, involved "trading for the account," every additional day of back contracts added to the $100,000,000 worth of July 30th would have stood in the way of a final settlement, and the reopening of the market (which was long postponed as it was) would have been much further delayed.

On August 4th, a problem which had loomed upon the horizon the day after the closing of the Exchange, was brought squarely before the Committee. A delegation of houses dealing in securities for European account appeared and stated that approximately $40,000,000 to $50,000,000 of securities were to arrive "this week, beginning to-morrow, Wednesday," and that they would be accompanied by sight drafts which would have to be financed. This alleged great volume of securities had been sold in this market for foreign account and borrowed in New York in order to make the immediate deliveries that our day to day system requires. The suspension of the fulfillment of contracts declared by the Exchange made it impossible to return this borrowed stock, and the houses doing this business were therefore obliged either to allow the drafts to go to protest or finance the incoming stock until the free enforcement of contracts was again permitted.

With money practically unobtainable, and general panic prevailing, it is needless to say that these statements of the delegation of houses doing foreign business were a severe shock to the Committee of Five. A remedy proposed by one or two of these banking houses was that the people from whom they were borrowing stock should be required to take it back. This simple expedient, while eminently satisfactory from the standpoint of the borrower of stock, was not very helpful to the Committee, as it would merely have shifted the problem of financing the stock from one set of brokers to another, and would have raised the dangerous question of a general enforcement of contracts in borrowed securities. It was an interesting illustration, among some others to be subsequently experienced, of the manner in which certain minds can become entirely absorbed in that aspect of a question which deals solely with personal interest. After careful discussion it was determined that the coöperation of the Clearing House banks should be sought in solving the difficulty. The Committee of Five thereupon sent a communication to the Bank Clearing House committee setting forth all the circumstances connected with the expected consignment of securities as stated by the delegation of banking houses and requested an appointment to meet them, or a sub-committee of their members, and discuss the matter. The appointment was obtained for the following morning, August 5th, and the Chairman and Mr. H. K. Pomroy were appointed a sub-committee to confer with the Bankers and directed to take Mr. Richard Sutro with them as a representative of the houses doing foreign business.

At the meeting with the Clearing House bankers it was very properly decided that a solution of the problem could only be reached when an exact knowledge of the amount of money required to pay for the incoming securities had been obtained, the figures stated by the banking houses which were seeking assistance being only estimates. The representatives of the Stock Exchange agreed to obtain this exact information at once, and having returned and stated the circumstances to the Committee of Five, it was directed that the following communication be sent to a list of members of the Exchange who, it was understood, were to have foreign drafts presented to them:—

> "The Special Committee of Five requests that by three o'clock to-day they may have in their possession from you information as to the number and amount of drafts which you expect will be presented to you from Europe on any steamers arriving to-day or subsequently. They would particularly like to know how much you expect on each steamer. In case any of these have already been financed please so state in your communication.
>
> "The Committee would also like to have you tabulate in your reply, so far as you can, the banks, trust companies or bankers from whom you expect drafts to be presented.
>
> "This communication is confidential and it is requested that you do not discuss this matter with any one outside your own firm. Your answer is expected by bearer, in order that the financing of these drafts may be facilitated."

By three o'clock, the same afternoon, replies had been received from thirteen houses that they expected securities on the *Olympic* and *Mauretania*, and had also received advices of other securities forwarded but did not know on what steamers; the drafts to be presented they said would be approximately for four and one half millions. Replies from twelve other houses stated it as a possibility but not a certainty that securities might reach them on the steamers above mentioned to the amount of about four millions; and, finally, twelve firms sent replies stating that they either expected no securities or had made the necessary arrangements to finance what was coming. These facts—so far below the estimate at first presented to the Committee—came as a great relief, and were at once taken before the Bank Clearing House Committee. After a careful discussion with these gentlemen the Committee of Five again met and sent the following communication to the firms who had reported that securities and drafts were about to be tendered to them.

> "Members of the Exchange to whom foreign drafts are presented for payment, are requested to confer with the Committee of Five at 9 A.M. to-morrow, Thursday, the 6th inst., in the Secretary's office, with details of such

transactions in hand, when efforts will be made to facilitate the adjustment."

The next morning the few firms who had drafts to meet on that day were provided with the necessary loans by two banks and a trust company at 8 per cent. The amount of securities due from Europe was undoubtedly large, but the great bulk of it had not been shipped and the shipment of it was postponed for many weeks afterward. The extraordinary statement that $40,000,000 or $50,000,000 were about to be landed in New York is interesting as showing the hysterical state of mind to which many business men had been reduced at that time. The actual amount of stocks sold to arrive, against which borrowings had been effected in New York, was finally shown to amount to $20,000,000. That this amount was not increased at an embarrassing period in these important negotiations was due in large measure to the action of the Committee in calling together the various foreign arbitrage houses, and securing from them an agreement to cable to their correspondents in Europe not to make further shipments of securities, because borrowed stocks could not be returned and deliveries effected. This as it turned out was an important step in the right direction.

Owing to the sudden and severe pressure of business to which the Committee of Five was subjected almost from the moment of its organization, some matters were unavoidably overlooked which should have had immediate attention. Conspicuous among these was the question of the rate of interest to be charged upon open contracts which the action of the Governing Committee had suspended. This matter was not reached until the meeting of August 4th, when the following ruling was made:

"The Special Committee rules that interest on the delivery at the rate of 6 per cent. shall accrue from August 5th on all unsettled contracts for delivery of securities, except that interest shall cease when a receiver of securities gives one day's notice to a deliverer that he is ready to receive and pay for same.

"The Special Committee further rules that sales of bonds on July 30th carry interest at the rate specified in the bond to July 31st, and that between July 31st and August 5th they are 'flat'; interest thereafter to be 6 per cent. on the amount of money involved, subject to the exemption stated in the previous ruling."

In view of the fact that no action had been taken up to August 4th and that a number of private settlements had been arranged in the meantime the Committee thought it wise to avoid a retroactive ruling, and imposed the 6 per cent. rate from August 5th. Injustice was done, in some cases, by permitting a lapse of five days when no interest charge was required, but this injustice was cheerfully borne owing to the unusual exigencies of the situation.

On this same day the Committee received the first communication which indicated that some members of the Exchange had not yet appreciated the necessities and dangers of the situation. This came in the form of a letter from the Baltimore Stock Exchange which contained the following passage:—

> "A representative New York Stock Exchange house has been guilty of going directly to one of the Trust Companies here, and made offerings of bonds dealt in on both your Exchange and our own, at a large concession."

The Committee directed the Secretary to make the following reply:—

> "In the matter of your letter of August 1, 1914, I am instructed by the Special Committee appointed by the Governing Committee on July 31, 1914, to inform you that in the opinion of said Committee the offering down of securities in places where money is loaned on securities is most reprehensible, and that members of this Exchange ought not to engage therein. If possible, I would like the name of the member of the New York Stock Exchange who made such offer."

It may be urged in extenuation of the act of the Stock Exchange house that, August 1st being only one day after the closing, a thorough appreciation of the gravity of the situation had not yet become general.

By August 5th the work of the Committee had assumed the form that was to continue unremittingly until the Exchange reopened four and one half months later. A constant stream of communications either by letter or by personal appearance filled the days sometimes from nine o'clock in the morning until six in the afternoon. The communications asked advice and made suggestions of every conceivable kind, but, above all, they were loaded with problems and difficult situations which had grown out of the breakdown of the financial machinery in general.

The labors of the Committee in striving to straighten out this formidable tangle of business affairs led to their issuing a series of rulings, which were binding upon all members of the Exchange. These rulings were sent over the "Ticker" whenever they were passed, but on August 5th it was decided to supplement the "Ticker" by distributing the rulings in circular form, and thus insure the possession by every member of a full copy of the entire number. It is a gratifying fact, both from the standpoint of the Committee and of the Stock Exchange, that no one of the very numerous rulings was a failure or had to be rescinded, and that they were all accepted without cavil or serious criticism by the members. In the relatively few cases where an indisposition to live up to these rulings was brought to the attention of the Committee, an appeal from them to loyalty and good judgment never failed to bring a recalcitrant member to terms.

On this day, August 5th, a special circular was sent out to answer the constant inquiries as to whether purchases or sales of securities were in any way permissible during the period of closing. It contained the following:

> "When the Governing Committee ordered the Exchange closed it was their intention that all dealings in securities should cease, pending the adjustment of the financial situation and the reopening of the Exchange.

> "It is possible that cases may occur where an exception would be warranted provided such dealings were for the benefit of the situation, and in no sense of a speculative character, or conducted in public. Any member, however, taking part in such transactions must have in mind, his loyalty to the Exchange, whether or not he is living up to the spirit of the laws, and that he is not committing an act detrimental to the public welfare."

On August 7th the question of the reopening of the Exchange again came to the front. A letter from Baltimore was received urging that the Exchange reopen for dealings in bonds only, and the newspapers were so urgent for some statement on the subject that the Committee authorized the following:

> "The Special Committee of Five will not recommend to the Governing Committee the reopening of the Exchange until in their judgment the financial situation warrants it, and as before stated, ample notice will be given of the proposed opening."

The question of borrowed and loaned stocks came up at this time in two aspects, one the interest rate to be charged, and the other the determination of the market price at which such loans should stand. With regard to the former the Committee ruled on August 5th that "until further notice, from and after this date, the interest rate on all borrowed and loaned stocks shall be 6%." In the latter case they ruled (August 10th) that "borrowed and loaned stocks must be marked to the closing prices on Thursday, July 30th, 1914, at the request of either party to the loan."

The effect of this second ruling was to establish the policy of regarding the closing prices of July 30th, as the market for securities, so that all loans, whether cash loans or stock loans, should be figured at this level. The making of any prices below those of July 30th was to be resisted by every available means, and the money-lending institutions were to be urged to coöperate by recognizing them as a basis for exacting margins. As long as this policy could be successfully carried out the danger of financial collapse would be averted.

It having been ruled that a lender of stock, by notifying the borrower of his willingness to take the stock back, could stop the interest charge on the contract, a considerable demand arose for new stock loans to replace those in which this privilege had been exercised. The matter of facilitating these new stock loans was taken up by the Stock Exchange Clearing House, and this together with the negotiations for voluntary settlement of back contracts now brought upon the Clearing House Committee that great volume of work which increased steadily until the reopening of the Exchange.

One step tending to increase this work was taken on August 11th, when the Committee ruled as follows:

> "Whenever a loaner of stocks gives one day's notice of willingness to have the same returned and the borrower fails to so return, the interest thereon shall cease. The Clearing House of the Exchange is prepared to advise and assist in making new stock loans and inquiries should be made in person there."

The effect of this ruling was to create a borrowing demand for stocks at current interest rates and the Clearing House Committee became the agency through which these stock loans were negotiated.

A further ruling, on August 11th, relative to the interest rate was to this effect:

> "That on all loans of stock made between members after this date the rate of interest is subject to agreement between the parties to the transactions, but should not exceed 6 per cent."

By the eleventh of August the question of the growth of an outside unregulated market began to force itself upon the attention of the Committee. All the organized Stock Exchanges of the country were closed, the auctioneers had loyally agreed to abstain from making sales, the "Curb" or recognized outside market was faithfully coöperating to prevent dealing, the unaffiliated bankers and money institutions were refraining even from the private sale of bonds in which they were interested, so that for a brief period there was a practically complete embargo on the marketing of securities. Naturally enough, so absolute a restraint brought on a pressure which was bound to force a vent somewhere. At first an occasional group of mysterious individuals were seen loitering in New Street behind the Exchange. A member of the Committee of Five, who was prone to see the humorous side of things even in those dark days, remarked as he observed them late one afternoon "the outside market seems to consist of four boys and a dog."

Before long, however, this furtive little group developed into a good sized crowd of men who assembled at ten o'clock in the morning and continued in session until three in the afternoon. At first they met immediately outside of the Exchange, but later they took up a position south of Exchange Place and close to the office of the Stock Exchange Clearing House. Their dealings increased gradually as time went on and never ceased entirely until the Exchange reopened. In all probability the existence of this market was a safeguard as long as its dimensions could be kept restricted. An absolute prohibition of the sale of securities, if continued too long, might have brought on some kind of an explosion and defeated the very end which it was sought to achieve.

This irregular dealing, as long as it remained within narrow limits and was not advertised in the press, furnished a safety valve by permitting very urgent liquidation. It was, however, continually accompanied by the great danger that it might grow to large and threatening proportions. If, in consequence of the facilities which these unattached brokers were offering, responsible interests should begin to take part in and help to create an open air market, the very disasters which the closed Exchange was intended to prevent might be brought about.

It was necessary, therefore, that the Stock Exchange authorities should do all in their power to hold the development of this market in check. With this end in view they not only prohibited their own members from resorting to it, but they exerted what influence they could upon others not to lend it their support. The banks and money lenders were urged not to recognize the declining prices which were established there as a basis for margining loans, as such recognition might tend to increase the dealings. One or two large institutions which, at first, were disposed to finance the operations conducted in the Street were persuaded to refrain from continuing to do so, and the press, while giving publicity now and then to the very low figures at which some leading stocks were quoted, was induced to avoid the practice of regularly tabulating these prices.

It having become apparent that some members of the Exchange, while obeying the mandate to do no trading in New Street, were indirectly helping the practice along by clearing stocks for the parties who were making the market there, the Committee ruled (August 11th) "that members of the Exchange are prohibited from furnishing the facilities of their offices to clear transactions made by non-members while the Exchange remains closed."

The final outcome was that the New Street market did more good than harm. It relieved the situation by facilitating some absolutely necessary liquidation, and never grew to such proportions as to precipitate disaster, but during the long suspense and uncertainty of the closing of the Exchange it was a constant and keen source of anxiety to the Committee of Five.

Toward the end of the first fortnight after the closing of the Exchange, the communications received by the Committee made it plain that there were quite a large number of purchasers, attracted by the low figures reached in the last day's trading, who were ready and anxious to buy securities at or above the closing prices. Obviously purchases of this kind by investors who happened to be in a position to take securities out of the market, promised to bring relief to interests whose position was critical and thus to fortify the general situation. This facility could not be extended in the form of a general permission to the members of the Exchange to make transactions privately at or above closing prices. To have permitted as far reaching a relaxation of restraint as this in so critical a time would have entailed too great a risk. If any one of the eleven hundred members had proved disloyal in the exercise of so dangerous a privilege and privately negotiated sales at prices below those of the closing, the whole plan of sustaining values might have been jeopardized.

After considering the matter very carefully the Committee concluded that the machinery and clerical force of the Stock Exchange Clearing House could be advantageously used to supervise and control transactions of this character, and, on August 12th, they issued the following ruling:

"Members of the Exchange desiring to buy securities for cash may send a list of same to the Committee on Clearing

House, 55 New Street, giving the amounts of securities wanted and the prices they are willing to pay.

"No offer to buy at less than the closing prices of Thursday, July 30, 1914, will be considered.

"Members of the Exchange desiring to sell securities, but only in order to relieve the necessities of themselves or their customers, may send a list of same to the Committee on Clearing House, giving the amounts of securities for sale.

"No prices less than the closing prices of Thursday, July 30th, 1914, will be considered."

Thus was established a market in the Stock Exchange Clearing House which was kept in operation until the complete reopening of the Exchange. Immense labor and difficulty were brought upon the Clearing House Committee in order to handle and supervise this unusual method of trading, and the extraordinary success with which it was carried through has entitled them to the lasting gratitude of their fellow members. The business was conducted by having a large clerical force tabulate the orders received and bring purchasers and sellers together who were willing to trade in similar amounts and at similar prices. In order to consummate a trade the Clearing House would notify both parties, leaving it to them to carry out the delivery and payment, and requiring them to inform the Clearing House when the transaction had been completed.

The first effect of furnishing this means for establishing a restricted market was very encouraging. A very considerable amount of business began at once to be entered into. Many people with ready money, who felt that securities had fallen to bargain prices, appeared as purchasers and relieved the necessities of those who had been embarrassed by the war crisis. A little later, however, when the progress of the war took on a more discouraging aspect, this "Clearing House Market" fell to the arbitrary minimum of the closing prices with a large excess of selling as compared to buying orders, and the "New Street Market" grew in proportion. During the darkest days of depression the prices of a few leading stocks such as U. S. Steel and Amalgamated Copper dropped in the Street ten points or more below their July 30th closings, and business in the Clearing House almost ceased, but in the later Autumn, when the rapid rise in the volume of American exports began to foreshadow a readjustment in foreign exchange, the New Street prices rose again to the Clearing House level and a relatively small business in the "outlaw" market was transformed into a relatively large business conducted under the supervision of the Exchange.

It is an interesting detail, worth mentioning, that the ruling of the Committee quoted above, which established a market in the Clearing House, used the permissive word "may" in stating that orders to buy and sell might be sent to that institution. This was soon taken advantage of by a few individuals who proceeded to conduct private transactions among themselves. Their excuse was that if transactions were merely permitted in the Clearing House it became optional as to whether they should take place there or elsewhere. Within a few days thereafter the Committee amended the ruling by substituting the word "must" for the word "may." The great responsibility attached to promulgating rulings, which were to be the law during this critical period, is made more apparent when it is realized that the ill considered use of a single word might bring on unforeseen and perhaps dangerous consequences.

During the month of August a constantly increasing pressure from every conceivable direction was exerted to break down the dam with which the Committee was striving to hold back the natural flow of dealings in securities. By letter and by personal appearance before the Committee individuals, in and out of the Exchange, strove to induce them to countenance transactions at prices below the arbitrary level of the closing. In addition to this agitation among individuals and firms, restlessness began to show itself in some of the other Exchanges. At one time the Stock Exchange of a great neighboring city, which had permitted restricted dealings exactly similar to those carried on in New York, wished to have those dealings regularly quoted in the newspapers; at another time a movement developed on the Consolidated Stock Exchange to establish some kind of restricted public dealing on their floor. The Committee of Five were obliged to labor hard and assiduously to hold this pressure back and keep the dam intact, and its efforts were ably and loyally seconded by the Committee of the Bank Clearing House whose great influence was unremittingly exerted to prevent the danger of premature action of any kind.

On September 1st the Clearing House banks were anxious to determine what was the amount, measured in money, of securities sold in New York by Europe and not yet received. The object of obtaining this information was to know what demand would be made upon the loan market if, at any time, these securities should be shipped. At the suggestions of the bankers the Committee of Five summoned before them representatives of all the houses doing a foreign business and requested them to send answers, as promptly as possible, to the following two questions:

First: "Amount due Europe for securities received to date and not yet paid."

Second: "Amount due Europe for securities already sold but not received from Europe."

On the following morning answers were handed in showing that the amount received and not yet paid for was $699,576.11, and that the amount due Europe on securities sold but not yet received was $18,236,614.15. The rapidity and accuracy with which this important information was obtained, without any publicity or disturbance of confidence, is interesting as showing the efficiency of the intimate coöperation between the banks and the Stock Exchange.

Among the many agencies for dealing in securities, whose activities were suddenly cut off on July 31st, the first in importance next to the Stock Exchanges themselves were the so-called bond houses. These firms, which included in their number many prominent private bankers, were dealers on a great scale in investment bonds, and when the thunderbolt of war struck they were carrying large lines of those bonds on borrowed money which, in the ordinary course of events, would have been placed among their numerous clients. When the crisis of early August had developed, all these houses (some of them not being members of the Stock Exchange) loyally coöperated in closing up the market, and abstained from negotiating their securities even in the most private manner. By the middle of August, however, a number of them began to show decided restlessness over the embargo upon their business. The cutting off of their accustomed income, while expenses continued as usual, was not what influenced them, for this hardship was shared by all Wall Street, but the enforced carrying of securities in bank loans at so critical a time when they felt that these securities might be disposed of became a grievance.

It was urged by many of them that the careful placing of these securities would be a great aid to the situation because every investor who made a purchase would facilitate the liquidation of their loans, ease the strain on the money market, and diminish the volume of securities for sale. There was undoubtedly much to be said in favor of this view when looked at from the standpoint of the effect upon the bond houses themselves or upon the loan market, but there was another aspect of the question which was less reassuring. If these houses started, at this terribly critical time, to place their securities among their clients at declining prices, and if these prices became known, which they certainly would, no one could foretell what the consequences might be. Many large institutions, such as Insurance Companies and Savings Banks, had funds invested in bonds, and many money lenders held loans upon bonds as security; what would be the effect upon these interests if a declining market even in unlisted bonds should be publicly quoted?

Influenced by this grave uncertainty the Committee of Five resisted the pressure brought upon them by certain representatives of the bond dealers who raised this question first on the nineteenth of August. Several of these gentlemen represented important firms and institutions which were not members of the Exchange, and their freedom from any obligation to be controlled by the Committee created a situation which threatened to become strained. In all cases of this kind, where an independent outsider and the Committee could not come to an understanding, the practice had become established of appealing to the Clearing House Bankers to act as a court of last resort. The banks, with their power to call loans, exerted an influence which could reach every nook and corner of the business world, and, at the same time, their immense facilities for feeling the financial pulse made them the best judges of what risks it was as yet safe to take. A series of meetings consequently took place between the Bank Clearing House Committee, the representatives of the bond houses, and the Committee of Five. At the first of these meetings the bank Presidents leaned very decidedly to the views of the Stock Exchange, and it was decided to postpone any consideration of a departure from the status quo for at least a fortnight.

The general situation remaining very critical all through August, no further steps were taken until September 8th. By that date a new factor had intruded itself into the situation. Certain corporate obligations were about to come due and the refunding of these obligations, whether in fresh issues of bonds or in short term notes, was going to make it necessary to withdraw the prohibition against placing investment securities upon the market. When this necessity became clear it was decided that some strict supervision and safeguarding of the sale of bonds and notes was necessary and the so-called "Committee of Seven," appointed by the bond dealers, were requested to formulate a plan for this purpose. This Committee of Seven consisted of members of the firms of: Brown Brothers & Co.; Guaranty Trust Co.; Harris, Forbes & Co.; Kissel, Kinnicutt & Co.; Wm. A. Read & Co.; Remick, Hodges & Co., and White, Weld & Co.

On September 9th, this Committee issued the following notice to bond dealers:

> "Your Committee is pleased to report that New York City's financial needs have been taken care of satisfactorily, thereby considerably clearing the foreign exchange

situation which existed when our communication of September 3d was sent out.

"The Committee is therefore of the opinion that the placing of securities owned by dealers with their private customers should be approved where the securities can be sold without disturbing the collateral loan situation and your Committee will be glad to continue to advise whenever such opportunities arise. Anything tending toward public quotations or the creating of the impression of an active or even semi-active market would unquestionably seriously disturb the loan situation.

"Transactions with bargain hunters should not be countenanced and your Committee will not approve the closing of transactions coming under this head. Prices should conform to the spirit which has prevailed during the past few weeks.

"Recognizing the support which banks and other lenders of money have given to dealers in securities, it should be the policy of such dealers when securities are sold to apply the proceeds toward the liquidation of loans.

"The Committee has considered questions of maturing obligations of cities and corporations and believes that the present situation does not warrant any attempt to issue long time bonds, but that such refunding should be accomplished through short time financing.

"The Clearing House Committee and the Stock Exchange Committee have expressed appreciation of the coöperation shown by the dealers in listed and unlisted securities and if all will endeavor to live up to the spirit of the policy thus far adhered to we are sure there will be no cause for criticisms on the part of the banks or the Stock Exchange Committee.

"Your Committee of Seven will continue to meet in the Directors' Room of the Chase National Bank daily, from 11 A.M. to 12 M., for advice on any cases where we can be of any assistance whatever."

The practical plan adopted was as follows:

Bond houses having securities of their own for sale could place them with their clients at prices approved by the Committee of Seven. All purchasers and sellers of bonds, acting as brokers only, were required to file their orders with the Committee of Seven when dealing in unlisted bonds, and with the Stock Exchange Clearing House when dealing in listed bonds, and these two agencies were empowered to determine minimum prices below which sales could not be made.

It will be seen that a very important step in the direction of relaxation of restraints was here taken. Not only was the prohibition of all dealings which had marked the beginning of the crisis withdrawn, but prices below the closing sales of July 30th were to be permitted subject to the supervision of a Committee.

As has already been stated, the Committee on Clearing House had their hands full from the time the Exchange closed, first with bringing about the settlement of the contracts of July 30th, and secondly with carrying on the business of making new contracts for members wishing to trade in securities at or above the closing prices. It was impossible, therefore, for the members of that Committee to give personal attention to the difficult problem of determining the prices below which listed bonds should not be sold. To meet this difficulty it was decided that a small additional Committee of men known to be thoroughly familiar with the bond business should be organized, and that it should be their duty to control the liquidation of listed bonds.

The carrying out of this plan at first met with a technical obstacle. The power to appoint a Special Committee rested exclusively with the Governing Committee of the Exchange; in order to secure action a special meeting of that body would have to be called; in the early weeks of September sentiment was still in so critical a state and every act of the Exchange was so keenly watched that it was feared the holding of an extraordinary meeting might start rumors and cause alarm. In view of these considerations the Committee of Five hit upon the makeshift of inviting three members of the Governing Committee, who possessed the desired qualifications, to volunteer their services as an advisory body in the matter of fixing prices for listed bonds. The three members selected were Messrs. C. M. Newcombe, Vice President of the Exchange, W. H. Remick, and W. D. Wood.

On the 19th of September these three gentlemen cheerfully undertook the difficult and onerous task urged upon them, and for three months they abandoned their own private interests and devoted their entire time to it. Owing to the intelligent and judicious manner in which they handled the delicate problem of conducting a liquidation in listed bonds that should at once be effective and yet not lead to demoralization, they placed themselves among the foremost of those to whom the financial community owes a debt of gratitude.

By the latter part of September methods, as described above, had been found for facilitating a restricted liquidation of listed stocks, and of listed and unlisted bonds. Nothing, however, had been done to make an outlet for unlisted stocks. The "Curb" market and certain prominent unaffiliated houses dealing in these securities had loyally played their part in suspending dealings, but symptoms began to show themselves of possible revolt, and the Committee of Five set to work to find a safety valve for this department also. The device of a supervisory Committee had proven so efficacious in other directions, that it was naturally turned to in this instance. The circumstances differed, however, in one particular. The bond dealers had spontaneously created for themselves the very efficient Committee of Seven who took their affairs in hand, but the interests involved in unlisted stocks did not show the same solidarity, and it was necessary for the Committee of Five to take a hand in initiating action.

With this end in view they consulted Mr. Herbert B. Smithers, of the firm of F. S. Smithers & Co., concerning the feasibility of having a committee formed to pass upon and control a resumption of dealings in unlisted stocks. Mr. Smithers was singled out for the reason that he was a member of the Stock Exchange whose firm was among the most prominent dealers in these securities, and the prompt and energetic way in which he undertook the task proposed to him soon convinced the Committee that they had not erred in resorting to him. He set about organizing a Committee at once and on September 24th he appeared before the Committee of Five accompanied by Messrs. A. C. Gwynne, F. H. Hatch, A. H. Lockett, and E. K. McCormick. These gentlemen announced that they were willing to act, with Mr. Smithers as their Chairman, and a plan for the control of the market in unlisted stocks was agreed upon.

In order to clothe this Committee (which included two Stock Exchange members, two representatives of prominent outside dealers, and the President of the Curb Association) with authority, the Committee of Five directed members of the Exchange to submit proposed dealings in unlisted stocks to them and abide by their rulings. The Stock Exchange Committee could, of course, only control its own members, but it being a fact that a very large part of the unlisted business emanated from Stock Exchange houses, it was probable that their action would determine that of unattached dealers. This expectation was, in the main, borne out, and business in unlisted stocks began to be carried on actively under the jurisdiction above described.

It is necessary to record, however, in the interest of preserving a correct picture of the happenings of this momentous time, that the smooth and gratifying operation of the various other Committees, which sprang into being to handle the numerous problems presented, was not entirely repeated in this case.

The conditions surrounding unlisted stocks seemed on the surface to be identical with those pertaining to unlisted bonds. In both cases a business that was partly in the hands of Stock Exchange members and partly in those of outside concerns was to be presided over by a mixed Committee representing both interests. In the case of the Bond Committee of Seven this supervision was accepted and cheerfully lived up to by practically all concerned. A different situation soon developed in unlisted stocks. Almost immediately certain individuals in the business began to assert that the unlisted Committee was a self appointed body which did not represent the people most concerned, and that being themselves dealers in the properties the trades in which were under their supervision, these gentlemen could not be trusted to act fairly in making their rulings. After much preliminary growling which vented itself in interviews with the Committee of Five, this antagonistic sentiment crystallized into a written protest.

On October 1st, the following statement was presented to the Committee of Five.

"GENTLEMEN:

"Owing to a general feeling of dissatisfaction amongst members and non-members of the New York Stock Exchange resulting from the formation of a Committee of Five to supervise dealings in Unlisted Securities, we, the undersigned, desire to suggest the following recommendations for your consideration:

"*First*: The personnel of the Committee be changed to the effect that same be composed of parties not identified as dealers.

"*Second*: That in stocks which have an open or active market, transactions may be made without restriction or necessity of report to the Committee, when at or above the closing prices of July 30, 1914.

"*Third*: That where securities have not had an active or open market the bid prices as published in the *Chronicle* of August 1st, be accepted as the closing prices.

"*Fourth*: That in the case of securities where the Committee may deem it possible to trade at prices below those prevailing on July 30th, they establish minimum prices good for as long a time as the Committee deems practical, and that a list of these prices be furnished to those making application for same."

"We think that if the above recommendations are put into force, it will do away with the criticism which has been made as to the Committee as at present constituted, and by so doing increase the efficiency of this Committee on Unlisted Securities, by securing thorough and hearty coöperation on the part of all brokers and dealers in these issues."

In reply to this appeal the Committee of Five pointed out that whenever, in other cases, the action of a Committee had been invoked to supervise the transaction of business, confidence in the integrity of that Committee had been general and unquestioned. The Committee of Seven, the Committee on Clearing House, the Committee of Three, and the Committee of Five themselves had all been vested with dictatorial powers over a business in which their members were personally engaged. In order to render trading in unlisted stocks a possibility, at the time, similar powers must be granted and similar confidence must be given to some one. The Unlisted Stock Committee were not self-appointed because they came into being at the instigation and suggestion of the Committee of Five, and to disband them after they had started upon their work, substituting other individuals in their places, would merely stimulate fresh antagonism that might wreck the entire project. The fact that these men were dealers in outside properties especially fitted them to pass upon the reasonableness of the prices that were to be made, and there was no more reason to question their integrity of purpose than there would be to doubt that of any individuals who might take their place.

A firm stand was thus taken in defence of this new Committee, and they succeeded in carrying on their work successfully up to the time when the amelioration of conditions enabled them to disband. It must be regretfully recorded, however, that the petty jealousy and distrust which had appeared in connection with this episode continued to show themselves in a desultory way until the end. A few individuals threw what impediments they could in the path of this Committee, and thereby furnished the only exception to the wonderful exhibition of loyalty and self effacement that manifested itself in every other department.

When the Exchange suddenly closed its doors, an immense number of people, consisting of employees of the Exchange itself and the clerical forces of all the many brokerage houses, were rendered idle. As soon as it became evident that the suspension of business was going to be indefinitely prolonged, the grave question arose as to the extent to which these people would be thrown out of employment. The Stock Exchange at once set the generous example of deciding to retain its entire force without reduction of wages, and this decision was carried through for the entire four and one half months of suspension. A more difficult problem, however, confronted the brokerage houses. Many of these firms had very heavy office rents and fixed charges of various kinds; their business had been showing meager profits and even losses for some years and, the length of the period of closing being impossible to forecast, they did not dare to undertake burdens that might get them into difficulties. The result was that a few strong houses, with philanthropic proclivities, carried their clerical forces through on full pay, but the majority were obliged to cut them down in various ways. In some cases the full force was retained on greatly reduced salaries, in others salaries were reduced and part of the force discharged, and the net result was that a great number of unfortunates were either thrown into unemployment altogether or placed in very straightened circumstances.

It is an interesting fact, bearing on the popular superstition that Wall Street is peopled by unprincipled worshippers of the dollar who are incapable of those finer qualities of character which are confined exclusively to other walks of life, that there is no region in which a quicker response to the call of the needy can be obtained than on the floor of the Stock Exchange. Even though the brokers were facing an indefinite period of starvation themselves, with expenses running on one side and receipts cut off on the other, the moment it became clear that severe suffering had come upon the clerical forces of the Street a movement was at once set on foot to start measures of relief and assistance. Perhaps the best way to convey an idea of the form which this assistance took is to quote from a report on the subject made by one of those who generously gave his time to the work. What follows is in his own words.

"A phase of the extraordinary and unprecedented conditions prevailing in the Financial District, commonly known as 'Wall Street,' was the necessity for cutting down office expenses, and though many firms carried their salary list intact, a considerable number laid off from one half to two thirds of their employees, and subsequent events developed the fact that some of them discharged practically their entire force.

"About the middle of September, the distress said to exist among the Wall Street employees, who had lost their positions as a result of the war in

Europe, prompted Mr. C. E. Knoblauch to suggest that some concerted action be taken to meet this emergency, if only as a temporary expedient. A number of informal discussions of the subject with fellow members of the Exchange, and further evidences of the existence of a wider field for the work than was at first realized, culminated in a call for a meeting in the office of Tefft & Company and immediate organization.

"Officers having been duly elected, the personnel of the Committee was declared to be as follows:—James B. Mabon, W. H. Remick, Graham F. Blandy, R. H. Thomas, W. W. Price, G. V. Hollins, C. E. Knoblauch, C. J. Housman, G. M. Sidenberg, Townsend Lawrence, T. F. Wilcox, Erastus T. Tefft, Chairman; Charles L. Burnham, Secretary; Edward Roesler, Treasurer.

"The title of the Committee was formally agreed upon as 'The Wall Street Employees' Relief Committee.'

"Through the courtesy of Mr. Clarence Mackey, the offer of a suite of rooms on the second floor of the Commercial Cable Building, 20 Broad Street, for the use of the Committee, at no charge for rent, was gratefully accepted, and arrangements for occupation were made at once. Mr. Oswald Villard, through a member of the Committee, evidenced his interest by offering temporary use of rooms in the *Evening Post* Building for the purposes of the Committee.

"It was determined that the principal object of the Committee would be to act as an Employment Bureau, to find positions for unemployed and to relieve distress where it was found to exist. It was understood and arranged for, that any Wall Street employee who had lost a position as a result of the war was eligible, and that no fees whatever be charged. A circular letter was sent to Stock Exchange members and firms appealing for subscriptions, and the matter of selection of a depository of the funds was referred to the Treasurer with power. The work of receiving and recording registration blanks commenced with a rush, over one hundred and fifty were filed the first day, and in a few weeks they numbered over one thousand.

"A very pleasant feature of the work was the cordial coöperation encountered on all sides. Helping hands were extended everywhere. The newspapers gave many 'reading notices,' and special advertising rates, and the news bureaus printed any and all notices as and when requested. The Stock Exchange Library Committee and the Secretary's Office placed their typewriting, multigraph and circular printing facilities at the Committee's disposal, furnished the rooms with desks, chairs, etc., and supplied all necessary stationery. The Stock Exchange force of telegraphers and other employees practically in a body volunteered their services, and those selected were of great assistance in preparing the card index system, which was used and found to be practical and eminently satisfactory. Appreciated assistance was promptly tendered by The Telephone Clerks' Association, The Association of Wall Street Employees, and The Wall Street Telegraphers' Association.

"Several cases of sickness, some very serious, were taken care of by Dr. L. A. Dessar, who gave free medical service to all applicants recommended by the Committee, and provided hospital treatment when required. The declarations made by the applicants demonstrated beyond any question that the number of men, women, girls and boys for whom prompt assistance in procuring employment was imperatively necessary had been greatly under-estimated, and evidenced an absolute argument endorsing the reasons for the Committee's existence.

"Many who applied were not in immediate need of money, but wanted employment, which the members of the Committee sought for them by individual solicitation of everyone they knew, or knew of, who were employers, and also by careful, judicious and timely advertising in the daily papers. Such satisfactory results were attained, that up to date of this writing, (May 15, 1915), of over seventeen hundred applications received, permanent positions were secured for about seven hundred at rates of compensation that were distinctly gratifying, all conditions considered. Two hundred and thirty were placed in temporary jobs for periods ranging from a few days to several weeks, a number of them being re-employed two or three times. Four hundred and ninety, having been taken back by their former employers, withdrew their applications.

"Numerous positions obtained for applicants while the Exchange was closed were in lines other than Stock Exchange business, and Wall Street clerks notwithstanding their recognized efficiency being, so to speak, specially trained, it was often found to be difficult, even impossible to make them fit the kind of work to which they were more or less strangers. In view of the fact that this circumstance made the accomplishment desired necessarily slow, the outcome demonstrated that it was reasonably sure.

"The request for subscriptions to the fund met with a hearty and generous response. Some apprehension was felt in this regard, but the splendid result proved to be an agreeable surprise. Appeals for subscriptions to the fund were made only to Stock Exchange members and firms, nevertheless, thanks to the general interest manifested, and the widespread advertising consequent thereto, contributions were received from generous friends outside of Wall Street, to an extent that was simply astonishing. Checks for $1,000 each were not unusual items, and as a rule the request was made, 'please do not publish my name.' A well known artist, in addition to a cash subscription, presented one of his paintings to the Committee. Through the kind assistance of the Chairman of The Stock Exchange Luncheon Club, the picture was sold for the substantial sum of $500.

"The Treasurer, with ample funds at his disposal, was able to meet calls for financial help that were frequent and pressing, and recognizing the desirability of experienced and competent assistance in making the necessarily intimate inquiries, to determine if applicants for relief were worthy, he applied to Mr. Robert W. DeForest, President of The Charity Organization Society, for expert advice in the matter, and was referred by Mr. DeForest to Mr. Frank Persons, Manager of the New York Bureau, and Miss Byington, in charge of the Brooklyn Branch, who rendered invaluable services in connection with many of the applications, all of which were carefully investigated. Much suffering and distress, and some cases of actual destitution were found to exist, and while a detailed statistical statement would seem uncalled for and not desired at this time, the following brief résumé of the Committee's 'relief work' will undoubtedly prove to be of interest.

"Financial assistance was extended to about one hundred individuals and families; rent was paid for thirty-nine; food purchased for forty-six; clothing was furnished in seven instances; five persons were placed in hospitals; there were a considerable number of cases where the Committee in whole or in part took care of funeral expenses; old debts for medical attendance and drugs; agency fees and surety bonds; life insurance premiums, board and lodging, etc., etc. Many applicants for assistance proved to be merely temporarily embarrassed, they were willing and anxious to be helped but did not want charity, so to meet that emergency a form of voucher was used, which acknowledged the receipt of a 'loan' without interest, to be repaid at the convenience of the 'borrower.' That applied to *cash* of course, payments for groceries, rent, etc., were simply receipted for.

"The results achieved, in the opinion of many, would seem to warrant an amendment to the original idea that a return to normal conditions would involve the dissolution of the Committee, and the proposition that it be made a permanent organization is being seriously considered."

This record is deeply gratifying to the brokerage fraternity because it discloses the fact that, even in the midst of a calamity so great that no individual could feel himself beyond the reach of insolvency, the impulse to succor the unfortunate remained as strong as ever among them.

CHAPTER III

THE REOPENING OF THE EXCHANGE

The fact that the Stock Exchange closed on July 31st and did not reopen fully until December 15th, might lead to the supposition that the question of reopening was not taken up before December. Far from this being the case, the truth is that reopening began to be discussed immediately after the institution was closed. Within twenty-four hours of the closing the minority, who had not been at first convinced of the wisdom of that action, joined with the majority in urgently advising that the Exchange be not reopened soon. All through the month of August a growing anxiety over the possibility of some hasty action by the Exchange authorities showed itself among brokers, bankers, and even some government officials. For this anxiety there was never any basis, because the officers of the Exchange having exceptional means of knowing what the dangers were, had no intention of assuming the immense responsibilities of re-establishing the market without the backing and approval of the entire banking fraternity. Gradually the excited solicitude about a premature reopening subsided as the ultra-conservative attitude of the Exchange was understood, and this was followed ere long by the first symptoms of agitation for the establishment of some form of restricted market.

As we have already shown the restraints of July 31st were relaxed one by one with the lapse of time. First a market at or above the closing prices was organized under the Committee on Clearing House; then Committees to facilitate trading in listed and unlisted bonds were formed; and finally a market was provided for unlisted stocks. All these devices, however, while they brought about readjustment and diminution of strain, did not constitute a reopening of the Stock Exchange, and the restoration of that great primary market, in some restricted way, became more and more a subject of public interest and concern.

As we have seen, the fundamental reason for closing the Exchange was that America, when the war broke out, was in debt to Europe, and that Europe was sure to enforce the immediate payment of that debt in order to put herself in funds to prosecute this greatest of all wars. To use an illustration popular in Wall Street at the time, there was to be an unexpected run on Uncle Sam's Bank and the Stock Exchange was the paying teller's window through which the money was to be drawn out, so the window was closed to gain time. How to reopen this window in such a way as not to pay out any more money to the foreign creditor than would suit our own convenience was the problem which soon began to agitate many ingenious minds. As time went on plans for performing this difficult feat poured in upon the Committee of Five in constantly increasing volume, and they were frequently accompanied by a request on the part of their authors that, when adopted, the credit for their success be publicly attributed to them. An edifying confidence was thus shown in what were usually the most visionary of these schemes.

Space does not permit the presentation of all these multitudinous suggestions, but as a matter of information we shall quote extracts from some of them. In point of time, the first communication to the Committee on this subject came on August 4th when a prominent banker appeared in person, and gave vent to the following oracular utterance: "When the Exchange reopens it should not do business from ten till three, but should open from ten o'clock to one. All transactions should be for cash, and must be delivered and paid for the same day, no contract to be allowed to stand over night." He also made the prediction, which was amply verified, that many weeks would elapse before the Exchange could be reopened at all. Some little time elapsed before anything further was presented on the subject, but by the end of August the flood of plans began and went on increasing until the Exchange resumed business.

On August 31st a communication was received from a well known "Statistical Organization" for "Merchants, Bankers and Investors" which said, in part: "In behalf of my clients, who are exceedingly interested in making it possible for the Stock Exchanges to open safely, I am getting the opinion of important bodies relative to the proposed legislation suggested on the enclosed slip, or any other which you think would serve the purpose." On the enclosed slip was the following proposed legislation "to enable the Stock Exchanges to open."

> "Be it enacted: That until the President considers European conditions fairly normal it shall be a misdemeanor in this country to buy, sell, transfer, give, or accept as collateral, shares of stock or evidences of indebtedness extending over one year, unless accompanied by a certificate showing that the owner is a United States citizen, together with such evidence as the Secretary of the Treasury may require that the securities have been owned by United States citizens since July 30th, 1914."

In answer to this proposition the Secretary of the Stock Exchange sent the following reply:

"Answering your letter of August 29th, 1914, I am instructed by the Special Committee of Five appointed by the Governing Committee to say that in its opinion such legislation as referred to would be ruinous to the credit of the United States throughout the world for many years to come."

In September a letter was received from a Western banker suggesting that the slogan "Buy a share of stock" if started "would achieve success, and by so doing would greatly benefit the stock market situation. This movement would have to be started so as not to create the impression among the many thousands of people it would reach, that it was merely a movement for the purpose of benefiting the stock brokers, but that it would be instrumental in relieving the strain on every conceivable business. Were such a movement accepted, and should it meet with results worthy of the plan it would be found out when the smoke clears away that American people would own American railway and industrial shares. This could be only for the great benefit of this country but for Europe as well, for the reason that if Europe knew that there was a good absorbing power here it necessarily would not dump its stocks at frightful sacrifices."

In October a junior member of one of the big private banking houses appeared personally and stated that, in his opinion, both domestic and foreign security holders should be treated alike; that sales should be conducted as usual; that on reopening transactions should be restricted and only sales be published and no bids or offers. His idea of restriction at the start was that all stock purchased should be paid for on the basis of 10% cash and the balance in certificates of deposit for cash, which certificates were to be non-negotiable except between banks. A Committee could, from time to time, remove the restrictions from such securities as seemed no longer to require them. The banks should be asked to agree not to call any present loans and to be very sparing in calling for margins.

Close upon the heels of this plan came a letter signed "A Friend of the People" which said "Let the Stock Exchange be opened strictly for the sale of American securities held by foreign stock holders. If they wish to throw their stocks over we can buy them at our own price. After six or eight days' selling from Europe the Exchange could be open to the world. By that time the market should be on a rising scale and safe for all."

This gentleman showed some originality in his view that the foreigner should be invited to sell at once, instead of being legislated out of the market as so many other advisers proposed. He seemed to be quite oblivious of the difficulties, however, that would have been encountered in inducing American security holders to stand by in pensive calm while the foreigners unloaded to their heart's content.

Early in November a Philadelphia banker wrote a long and intricate letter the full details of which we have not space to reproduce, but it contained the following fragment which is interesting in its way:

> "Could not a plan be formulated between the Stock Exchanges, investment bankers and Federal Reserve Banks, by which the securities could be valued on their intrinsic and market values at such prices that would be considered reasonable to be obtained in the next two or three years; that the lenders be guaranteed against any losses from recession below the stipulated point at which the securities might later be liquidated, say sometime during the year 1917, if it had not been voluntarily liquidated without loss before. Loans so insured would have to be in force on securities carried prior to a certain date, probably before the Exchange opened, if not last July 30th, and that an insurance premium would be charged which would be considered slightly more than adequate. Any surplus could be eventually pro-rated to the policy holders. There would need to be no obligation to take out such insurance unless the borrowers preferred. The banks might, however, force them to do so in many cases or pay off loans."

At about this time many letters and suggestions were received centering round the main idea that the market be opened exclusively for such stocks as were not much held in Europe. Just as a correspondent cited above seemed to believe that American security holders could be compelled to remain inactive while foreigners sold their holdings, so these people imagined that holders of one class of securities could be kept quiet while the prices of some other class were declining in a free market.

With the above came a letter from a correspondent whose thoughts carried him back to the old days of buyers' and sellers' options, when most of the security business was done on 30 or 60 day contracts. He proposed that the Exchange be reopened so that "all trades made be 'buyer 60'. No other bids or offers to be valid." This would postpone for two months the settling day for the expected liquidation, and he felt certain that by that time there could be no trouble in meeting obligations. Unfortunately at the time he wrote there was no way of obtaining assurance of this happy outcome. The same idea in a somewhat different form came from another correspondent who, instead of deferring payment by a buyer's option, proposed that stocks and bonds be sold on a 10 per cent. basis "That is, the seller of 100 shares of Union Pacific at 112 will deliver to buyer 10 per cent. of amount sold, and receive a check for $1,120, together with a contract in which the buyer agrees to take 10 per cent. more, or say 10 shares at the end of six months, 10 shares in 9 months, 10 shares in 12 months, 10 shares in 15 months," etc., etc., at the original price of $112 per share. This plan seemed to contemplate a bequest of unsettled contracts to future generations of unsuspecting brokers. The author of it was particularly solicitous that, in the event of its adoption, his name should be handed down to posterity along with the unfulfilled contracts.

An idea of very wide prevalence, which was touched upon in nearly all communications to the Committee and which even some bankers approved, was that a preliminary step to reopening should be an agreement by the banks not to call loans made prior to July 31st, 1914, for some specified period of time. This idea was very thoroughly discussed and looked into by the Committee. It was found to present great practical difficulties, but was never definitely abandoned until the resumption of business was shown to be possible without it.

The advice which was received by the Committee of Five with regard to reopening was divided into two classes. There was that large body of suggestions, some of which we have described above, which were volunteered either in letters or in interviews, and there was the advice of well known bankers and men of financial prominence which the Committee itself solicited. In the latter class figured a member of one of the largest private banking houses in New York whose opinions and counsel were of inestimable value. This gentleman, gifted with clear insight and a thorough grasp of the situation, and generously anxious to be of service to the Committee, pointed out from the start that the reopening of the Exchange hung upon a favorable swing in the balance of trade. When the indebtedness of the United States to Europe could be offset by our exports the danger of reëstablishing our market would become negligible, and this shrewd adviser predicted that the desired reaction in foreign exchange was much closer at hand than was generally supposed. The most valuable of his admonitions, and the words which did most to strengthen the courage and resolve of the Committee were these: "You will be given all kinds of advice by all kinds of people, but remember that in the end the responsibility will fall upon you, therefore listen attentively to everything you are told but act on your own independent judgment." This wise course was successfully followed, and the change in the trend of foreign exchange came, as he predicted, much sooner than was expected.

Numerous other prominent men who were turned to for assistance showed the greatest willingness to render every service within their power, and placed the Committee under heavy obligations. There was one case where the zealous desire to work out a very detailed solution of the reopening problem brought a ray of humor into these otherwise serious and anxious discussions. A certain private banker presented his scheme in approximately the following words: "Before you can reopen the Exchange you must be in a position to know to what extent Europe is going to throw our securities upon this market, and the only way to obtain this information is to send some members of your Committee abroad. This delegation should go first to London and settle there for a long enough time to get intimately acquainted with leading persons in the financial world. This could be done by cultivating social intercourse, dining and consorting with these people until a frank statement from them could be obtained concerning the probable volume of American securities for sale."

As this statement proceeded visible signs of painful emotions manifested themselves among the Committee. The Exchange had already been closed three months, and they were being informed that a plan requiring a lapse of some six months more must be carried out before the happy day of resumption would be in sight. The banker having paused for a few minutes' reflection, resumed: "Then there is France. Many American securities are held there, and as under their system the action of individual investors is largely controlled by the financial institutions, it will be quite feasible to determine the probable selling of French investors when you have got in intimate touch with these institutions." Another additional six months' delay loomed to the vision of the demoralized Committee, and sad words of reproachful protest were about to burst from some of them when their mentor again broke the chilly silence of the meeting room. "Now that I think of it there is Switzerland. The Swiss are a thrifty and saving people and undoubtedly have much money in our properties. In spite of her neutrality Switzerland will feel the economic pinch of this war and her people will have to liquidate many of their foreign holdings. It will be wise, therefore, for you to extend your inquiries from France into Switzerland."

Here the reaction came, the heart-sick feeling which had plunged the respectfully attentive Committee into gloom vanished, and mirthful emotions so possessed them that it was a hard task to maintain proper dignity and decorum. The temptation to inquire whether this contemplated trip around the globe was to include an effort to trace some American railroad bond into the sacred precincts of Thibet, or a dash to the South Pole to search the abandoned luggage of some deceased explorer, was resisted, and the worthy banker whose imagination had taken such distant flights retired unconscious of the very mixed emotions he had aroused. In the light of the actual reopening that took place only six weeks later this interview becomes a curiosity worth preserving.

—————————————————

Along with other prominent men who consented to meet and consult with the Committee there came Sir George Paish and Mr. Basil G. Blackett. These two gentlemen had come over from England to consult our government and our banking fraternity with regard to the abnormal exchange situation created by the outbreak of war. Before the Committee of Five they, of course, dwelt mainly upon the question of reopening the market. Sir George Paish, being by nature an optimist, took a very roseate view of the outlook, so much so that some members of the Committee were at first disposed to fear (his mission being that of a collector of debts who sought prompt payment) that his diagnosis of the situation was prompted more by his hopes than by his convictions. He proceeded to Washington, where he spent a considerable time negotiating with the national authorities, and on his way home he again appeared before the Committee, on November 23rd, and stated his belief that the Exchange could be reopened at once.

In the light of what followed it is plain that Sir George Paish's views were very nearly correct and not by any means over-optimistic. The rapidity with which the readjustment of exchange solved the problem presented to the American market was entirely in harmony with his predictions and very flattering to his judgment. His companion, Mr. Basil G. Blackett, was a reticent young man who seldom intruded himself into the discussion, but it was noticeable that whenever he was asked for an expression of opinion he showed himself to be thoroughly informed as to facts and sound in judgment. The Committee was certainly under an obligation to these gentlemen for the time they were willing to give to its deliberations. In this connection it is a pleasure to record that the authorities of the London Stock Exchange showed a similarly friendly disposition. All through the period of crisis communications passed between the London and New York Exchanges and were accompanied by a most friendly spirit of mutual assistance.

—————————————————

While plans for reopening the Exchange were discussed from an early date, nothing definite took shape up to the end of October, and at that time the Committee of Five were still in the dark as to how long business would continue to be suspended. Whether the New Year would find Wall Street still bound and muzzled was an open question on November 1st. As the month advanced, however, a very rapid change in conditions began to manifest itself. On November 10th two significant steps were taken. Mr.

Smithers, Chairman of the Unlisted Stocks Committee, appeared and stated that his Committee intended making a report recommending their own discontinuance. He was followed, on the same day, by Mr. E. R. McCormick, Chairman of the Board of Representatives of the Curb Market Association, who urged that the time for a formal reopening of the Curb was at hand. On the following day the Committee on Unlisted Stocks, having submitted a proposed circular which they wished to issue in announcement of their dissolution, the Committee of Five adopted the following rule:

> "The Special Committee of Five being of the opinion that the market for unlisted stocks has arrived at a condition that makes supervision of dealings no longer necessary, hereby approve the act of the Committee on Unlisted Stocks in dissolving their organization.

> "Ruling No. 23, dated September 24, 1914, is hereby rescinded."

It is needless to say that this action, together with its ratification by the Committee of Five, was first submitted to and approved by the Clearing House banks. Unlisted stocks comprised a group of properties which were practically not held abroad, and the reason for holding them under close restraint at first was the danger of the sentimental effect on a panicky situation in case their prices should undergo a violent decline. It having been demonstrated that such a decline was not to be feared, the Committee in charge were only too glad to relinquish the difficult duty of supervising the trading and open a free market. It was further decided that the restraint upon free quotation and publication of prices be simultaneously removed from the unlisted dealings.

As a natural sequence to the above action, on November 12th, the Curb Association issued the following notice:

> "To the Members of the New York Curb Market Association:

> "GENTLEMEN:

> "It has been decided that the improvement in the general financial situation has removed the necessity for restrictions over trading in unlisted stocks, therefore you are hereby notified that the New York Curb Market will officially resume business on Monday, November 16th, 1914, at 10 o'clock A.M.

"This action on the part of the Chairman of the New York Curb Market Association has received the approval and sanction of the Committee of Five of the New York Stock Exchange.

"E. R. McCormick,
"*Chairman.*"

On November 13th, the Committee of Five ruled that:

"Unrestricted trading in Listed Municipal and State Bonds for domestic account may now be resumed, but that all transactions for future delivery must be submitted for approval, as heretofore, to the Sub-Committee of Three on Bonds at the Clearing House of the New York Stock Exchange."

On November 16th, Mr. Frank W. Thomas, Vice-President of the Chicago Stock Exchange and also Chairman of their "Trading Committee," appeared before the Committee of Five and stated that it was the intention of the authorities of their Exchange to meet on the coming Wednesday to discuss the advisability of opening on Monday, November 23rd. He asked for information regarding the attitude of the New York Stock Exchange in the matter of securities listed on both exchanges. The Committee requested him not to permit dealings in Chicago, in such securities, at prices below the minimum prices established in New York.

Thus one after another came the evidences of a sudden transformation in the financial conditions and of a consequent movement toward the resumption of business, all of which rested fundamentally on an immense increase of our exports and the resulting favorable movement of foreign exchange.

Encouraged by these happenings the Committee of Five actively took up numerous plans for letting down the bars. There had been for some time considerable pressure exerted by those members of the Exchange who were distinctively bond brokers, to have the bond business transferred from the Clearing House to the floor of the Exchange. They thought that this step would make a wider and more satisfactory market for bonds and that the supervision of the Committee of Three could be exerted in one locality as well as in the other. In view of the rapid improvement in conditions, and the fact that unlisted bonds had been given an unrestrained market by the dissolution of the Committee of Seven, it was thought that the moment had come for taking this step in advance. Preparations were at once set on foot to restore the restricted bond market to the floor and thereby insure that partial opening of the doors of the Exchange which would be the entering wedge to ultimate resumption.

———

Unfortunately the plans of the Committee in this regard were not sufficiently safeguarded. Through some unforeseen leak the news of their intentions got abroad, and brought on some awkward consequences. The first of these was the appearance of a private banker, the same one who early in August had predicted a long period of suspension, to protest against greater freedom in bond dealings. He foresaw terrible results if this rash act were permitted and claimed to have information that European holders of bonds were awaiting this chance to swamp the market. The Committee were not much alarmed by this gentleman's warnings and were proceeding with their nefarious scheme when a further warning was addressed to them. There was a certain member of a Stock Exchange firm who was on friendly terms with some of the Washington authorities, and who seems to have felt it his duty to see that the Exchange did nothing to give offense in these high quarters. When this individual learned what the Committee had in mind he sent word that it would be prudent for them to let a particular government officer know their plans before putting them into execution. Thinking that this warning must be based on some special information the Committee at once authorized this gentleman to inform his friend in the Government of their plan. This was on Wednesday, November 18th, and the intention of the Committee was to place the bond market upon the floor of the Exchange on the following Monday. On Thursday this well meaning but somewhat misguided go-between reported that he had communicated with Washington and that his friend there had expressed the desire to see some member of the Committee before any further steps were taken.

This news hit the plans of the Committee somewhat after the manner of a submarine torpedo. They had everything in readiness for Monday, and the newspapers, which had also got wind of their intentions, had already announced to the public unequivocally that a restricted bond market would be started on that day. With such limited time to act in there was nothing to resort to but postponement and a notice was immediately given to the press in the following words:

> "The Special Committee of Five states that while the plan outlined by the newspapers concerning a further extension of the present method of dealing in bonds was substantially that under consideration by the Committee, the magnitude of the interests affected has led to unforeseen difficulties which will necessitate further

consideration. When a decision is reached ample notice will be given to the public officially."

A letter was at once sent to the Government official notifying him of the readiness of the Committee to visit him at his convenience, and the following day, Saturday, he very courteously sent them a telegram explaining that the suggestion of an interview had in no way emanated from him but that he had misunderstood the intermediary (who had communicated by telephone) and supposed that the interview was being sought by the Exchange. So this mighty tempest in a tea pot resulted from the excessive zeal of an outsider who while trying to pilot the Committee into safe waters succeeded in running it on a reef of his own creation.

Immediately on ascertaining the true situation the following notice was sent out on Saturday:

> "The Special Committee of Five announces that having consummated its plan for bond transactions on the Exchange under certain specified restrictions, the same will, in accordance with the Constitution of the Exchange, be submitted to the Governing Committee at the regular meeting to be held on the 24th inst. If the recommendations of the Special Committee are adopted by the Governing Committee the plan will go into operation at an early date."

Some of the newspapers having announced positively that this new move with regard to bonds would take place on Monday, the 23rd, they were very indignant that it should be postponed without supplying them with a good and sufficient reason. The Committee, on its part, feeling that it was undesirable to publish the details of an awkward misunderstanding with a public official, who would not want his name dragged into a matter that he had in no way concerned himself with, refused to furnish the reason. This at once let loose upon them those vials of reportorial wrath which, up to that time, they had been fortunate in escaping. One journal amicably stated that this incident merely emphasized a fact which had all along been obvious, namely that the Committee were, and had been from the start, totally incompetent to perform the task intrusted to them.

While a gentle shower of epithets fell upon their devoted heads the Committee proceeded with their work and, having obtained the necessary authority from the Governing Committee, they sent out the following ruling on November 24th:

> "That so much of rule No. 21 as applies to dealings in listed bonds through the Clearing House be rescinded, to

take effect at the close of business on Friday, November 27th, 1914. Beginning on Saturday, November 28, 1914, dealings in bonds listed on the Exchange will be permitted on the floor of the Exchange between the hours of ten and three o'clock each day except Saturday, when dealings shall cease at twelve o'clock noon. Such dealings to be under the supervision and regulation of the Committee, and to be for 'cash' or 'regular way' only and not below the minimum prices as authorized by the Committee from time to time. Transactions at prices other than those allowed by the Committee, or in evasion of the Committee's rules, are prohibited. All rules of the Exchange governing delivery and default on contracts covered by this resolution shall be in force on and after Saturday, November 28th, 1914, but the closing of contracts 'under the rule' shall be subject to the foregoing provisions."

Thus on Saturday, November 28th, the doors of the Stock Exchange were once more thrown open and a restricted market in listed bonds was established on the floor under the watchful eye of the Committee of Three. There was some hesitancy at first as to whether these bond transactions should be quoted on the ticker in the accustomed way, but before the day of opening came it was decided to report them as usual. By requiring that all trades should be for "cash" or "regular way" and, in a subsequent ruling, by instructing all purchasers of bonds to report to the Committee when such bonds were not delivered by 2.15 P.M. on the day following the purchase, it was hoped to impede any sudden or violent liquidation of foreign securities.

———————

The restoration of the bond market to the floor was a complete success, and at about the same time a general revival of public confidence showed itself in a rise in prices first in the street market and then in the Stock Exchange Clearing House itself. Encouraged by these symptoms the Committee of Five at once formulated a plan for carrying the reopening a step farther. A list of stocks which were not international in character was made out and submitted to the Bank Clearing House Committee, and with their concurrence it was decided to place these upon the floor of the Exchange to be traded in at or above certain prescribed minimum prices.

At a meeting of the Governing Committee on December 7th the following resolution was adopted: "That the Committee of Five is hereby empowered to permit dealings on the floor of the Exchange in such stocks as it may designate under restrictions prescribed by it. That the Committee of Five is hereby authorized to enforce stock loan contracts whenever in its judgment it may deem best so to do, and that the resolution of July 31st, 1914, be modified in this respect."

A list of minimum prices was fixed upon that averaged some two or three points below the closing prices of July 31st, and on December 11th the Committee issued a ruling prescribing the conditions for the partial resumption of stock dealings on the Exchange. We here present it in full:

> "The Special Committee of Five rules that Rule 13 be rescinded, in so far as it applies to stocks admitted to dealings in the Exchange from time to time by the Committee of Five, said rescission to take effect at the close of business on Friday, December 11, 1914.
>
> "Beginning on Saturday, December 12, 1914, dealings in certain specified stocks listed on the Exchange will be permitted on the floor of the Exchange between the hours of ten and three o'clock each day except Saturday, when dealings shall cease at twelve o'clock noon.
>
> "Dealings in such stocks as shall be specified by, and be under the supervision and regulation of the Committee, shall be for 'cash' or 'regular way' *only* and not below the minimum prices authorized by the Committee from time to time. Transactions at prices below those allowed by the Committee, or in evasion of its rules are prohibited.
>
> "A list of stocks to be admitted to dealings on the Exchange accompanies these rulings. Minimum prices on same will be announced on December 11, 1914.
>
> "All stocks quoted on July 30th at or below 15 per cent., or $15 per share, may be dealt in without restriction as to price, but are included in the list for your guidance, and will be marked 'Free' in the price column.
>
> "All stocks admitted to dealings as above, which were being cleared through the Stock Exchange Clearing House at the close of business on July 30, 1914, will be similarly cleared from the opening of business on the 12th day of December, 1914.
>
> "All stocks admitted to dealings, which were being dealt in 'Ex-Clearing House' at the close of business on July 30,

1914, will be similarly dealt in from the opening of business on the 12th day of December, 1914.

"Stocks admitted to dealings on the Exchange will cease to be dealt in through the Stock Exchange Committee on Clearing House. Stocks not so admitted will continue to be dealt in through the Committee on Clearing House until further notice.

"All rules of the Exchange governing delivery and default on contracts covered by these rules shall be in force on and after the 12th day of December, 1914, but the closing of contracts 'Under the Rule' shall be subject to the foregoing provisions.

STOCKS LOANED

"The Loan Market for stocks will reopen at ten o'clock, A.M. on the 12th day of December, 1914, for such stocks *only* as are admitted to dealings on the Exchange, from and after which date all rules of the Exchange governing the borrowing and loaning of such stocks shall be in force, but the closing of contracts 'Under the Rule' shall be subject to the foregoing provisions.

"The above rule shall apply to stocks borrowed and loaned prior to and since July 30, 1914.

"Borrowed and loaned stocks will be cleared as before July 30th last, but only in cases where such stocks are admitted to dealings on the Exchange.

"Loans of stocks *not* admitted to dealings on the Exchange will continue to stand until further notice, unless otherwise agreed to by both parties to the contract."

On Monday, December 14th, the next business day after the limited list of stocks had been placed upon the floor of the Exchange, it was reported to the Committee that the volume of transactions taking place in the Stock Exchange Clearing House, in the stocks not yet admitted to the floor, had risen to such proportions as seriously to embarrass that institution. As this activity was taking place on a rising market and signs of increasing confidence were constantly multiplying, the Committee quickly resolved, on the same day, to transfer all stocks to the floor on the following morning, and notice to that effect was at once sent out. The unexpected appearance of this notice on the tape was greeted with cheers of approbation in the Exchange, and on December 15th the long hoped for reopening of the entire market had become a reality.

The Committee of Five by this act brought their own rule to a close. Arbitrary power had been put in their hands to be exercised while the Exchange remained closed, but now that it was reopened authority naturally returned to its legitimate channels. The Committee therefore presented the following report to the Governing Committee on December 15th:

> "The Special Committee of Five beg leave to report that in as much as the crisis that existed on July 31st, 1914, has passed, and financial affairs in this country have resumed a practically normal condition, the necessity for the Committee's continuance no longer exists and hence they request to be discharged. Before being discharged they desire to express their appreciation of the trust and confidence placed in them by the Governing Committee. They also wish to express to the members of the Exchange their appreciation of the manner in which their rulings have been respected, even though in many cases it involved great sacrifices.
>
> Resolved, That the report of the Special Committee of Five be received, and the Committee be discharged."

Thus, like the sudden and unexpected shifting of a dream, the Committee of Five who so recently had almost despaired of fixing a date for reopening the Exchange, found the Exchange open and themselves a memory of the past. The abruptness of their exit was tempered, however, in the following manner. As above described, the reopening was accompanied by the restraint of certain arbitrary minimum prices below which securities could not be sold. It was felt that, owing to the critical and indecisive state of the war, there was a continuing possibility of some news that might renew a crisis in the market. While this possibility lasted the maintenance of minimum prices furnished an automatic check upon sudden panic which would avoid raising the question of a second closing of the Exchange. In order to regulate these minimum prices and so change them from time to time as to keep in accord with normal supply and demand, it was necessary to appoint a Committee, and the original Five were continued in office with this sole regulative power. As bonds were similarly restricted, the Committee of Three also lingered on the scene for the same purpose. The two Committees performed this unusual function up to the first of April,

1915, when the very marked improvement in conditions led to the abandonment of this last vestige of artificial restraint.

It is instructive, as showing the workings of some minds, that although the Committee of Five, in its capacity of regulator of minimum prices, issued a public statement that they were under no circumstances going to valorize or sustain prices but merely expected to maintain a safeguard against some unforeseen shock to confidence, many people wrote them urgent letters asking that in certain properties a minimum should be maintained which would render selling impossible. It was quite futile to try to disabuse some of these correspondents of the idea that no decline should be allowed in properties that they were interested in.

To one who meditates upon the singular experience which was thus abruptly brought to a close, there are a few features of it which stand out as meriting the especial attention of all members of the Stock Exchange. First of all it was most impressively shown what apparently hopeless tasks can be accomplished by loyal coöperation. If at any time up to July, 1914, any Wall Street man had asserted that the stock market could be kept closed continually for four and one-half months he would have been laughed to scorn, and yet this supposed impossibility was performed by the joint and determined action of the financial community. On the other hand, and as a counterpart to this valuable experience, it must never be lost sight of that the extraordinary war measures of 1914 may be a danger to the future if they are misinterpreted. There is a possibility (even a probability) that when ordinary crises arise in times to come, people who find themselves financially embarrassed will bring enormous pressure upon the authorities of the Exchange to renew the drastic expedients of the famous thirty-first of July. It is to be sincerely hoped that there will always be firmness enough in the Governing Committee to resist this pressure. The great world war coming, as it did, without warning was a rare and epoch-making event that warranted unheard of action and to indulge in such action for any lesser cause would be utterly disastrous.

The Committee of Five seems to have been brought into existence under a lucky star. That five men called together so suddenly in such an emergency should have worked with absolute harmony for so long a time is quite remarkable. Their unanimity was never troubled but once. On one of the first few days of their career a rather positive and aggressive member, arguing with a colleague, said "you must remember that you are only one of this Committee." The Committeeman thus addressed responded with calm determination "and you must not forget that you are not the other four." This encounter excited much amusement among the remaining members and was the one and only occasion where anything resembling a serious difference appeared.

In addition to being blessed with harmony they were very fortunate in having passed rulings for so long a time without giving forth anything that had to be recalled. In view of the complexity of the conditions, fortune must have aided in this as well as judgment. They were, of course, treated to much wisdom (after the event) by their critics. They were told that they might have opened the Exchange sooner after the actual opening had proved a success, and they were informed in the editorial columns of a prominent journal that their fear of foreign liquidation had been an "obsession" which lacked justification. These critics never were heard from while the event was in doubt, and consequently the Committee did not profit much by their learned sayings.

It can be stated with confidence that the intelligent resourcefulness of the Stock Exchange, in conjunction with the splendid public spirited work of the New York banks and the press, warded off a calamity the possible magnitude of which it would be difficult to measure. The success of this undertaking should be a source of pride and emulation to those future generations of brokers who will have to solve the problems of the great financial market when in the words of Tyndall, "you and I, like streaks of morning cloud, shall have melted into the infinite azure of the past."

THE END

Lightning Source UK Ltd.
Milton Keynes UK
UKHW010647291222
414571UK00004B/173

9 789356 784819